FACT CAT

LIGHT

Sonya Newland

WAYLAND
www.waylandbooks.co.uk

FACT CAT

Get your paws on this fantastic new
mega-series from Wayland!

Join our Fact Cat on a journey of fun
learning about every subject under the sun!

First published in Great Britain in 2017 by Wayland
Copyright © Hodder and Stoughton Limited, 2017

All rights reserved
ISBN: 978 1 5263 0174 1

10 9 8 7 6 5 4 3 2 1

MIX
Paper from
responsible sources
FSC® C104740

Wayland
An imprint of Hachette Children's Group
Part of Hodder & Stoughton
Carmelite House
50 Victoria Embankment
London EC4Y 0DZ

An Hachette UK Company
www.hachette.co.uk
www.hachettechildrens.co.uk

A catalogue for this title is available from
the British Library
Printed and bound in China

Produced for Wayland by
White-Thomson Publishing Ltd
www.wtpub.co.uk

Editor: Sonya Newland
Design: Clare Nicholas
Fact Cat illustrations: Shutterstock/Julien Troneur
Consultant: Karina Philip

Picture and illustration credits:
Alamy: Jochen Tack 19; Stefan Chabluk: 14; iStock: Good-
LifeStudio 6t, lilyling1982 7, AVTG 8, shalamov 9, ranplett
10, monkeybusinessimages 17, Szabolcs Takacs 20; Shutter-
stock: rangizzz 4–5, Patrick Foto 4, somchaij 5, Cathy Keifer
6b, design56 11l, Amero 11mt, Roman Yastrebinsky 11mb,
onzeptm 11rt, threeseven 11rb, Zurijeta 12, Marcin-linfernum
13, Dvarela 15, Milen Kanev 16, fuyu liu 18, Dr_Flash 21.

Every effort has been made to clear copyright.
Should there be any inadvertent omission,
please apply to the publisher for rectification.

**The author, Sonya Newland, is a writer and editor
specialising in children's educational publishing.**

**The consultant, Karina Philip, is a teacher and
a primary literacy consultant with an MA
in creative writing.**

FACT CAT FACT

There is a question for you
to answer on every spread
in this book. You can check
your answers on page 24.

CONTENTS

WHAT IS LIGHT?

Light is important to all living things. Without **sunlight**, there would be no plants, animals or people on Earth.

Plants and flowers need light to grow strong.

You use light in many ways. Television and computer **screens** light up so you can see them. Lights tell you when it is safe to cross the road.

Lighthouses send **beams** of light out to sea to warn ships when there are rocks close by.

FACT CAT FACT

Light looks white, but it is really made up of different colours. You can see these when light shines through raindrops and makes a rainbow. What are the colours of the rainbow?

SOURCES OF LIGHT

Light comes from different **light sources**. Some sources are **natural**. The Sun, **lightning** and fire are all natural sources of light.

Lightning is a bright flash of light in the sky during a thunderstorm.

FACT CAT FACT

Fireflies are insects that make their own light in their bodies. What type of worm makes its own light?

Other light sources are **man-made**. Torches, lamps and candles are sources of light that are made by people.

Fireworks are a man-made light source. Light from fireworks can be many different colours.

SUNLIGHT

The Sun is our biggest source of light. It sends out light in all **directions** through space. Some light eventually reaches Earth.

Light always travels in straight lines. You can see the lines as the Sun shines through these trees.

FACT CAT FACT

It takes 8 minutes and 20 seconds for light from the Sun to reach Earth. Find out how far away the Sun is from Earth.

Light from the Sun is incredibly bright. It only takes a few seconds for sunlight to harm your eyes. You should never look directly at the Sun.

You can protect your eyes when out in bright sunshine by wearing sunglasses and a hat.

LIGHT AND MATERIALS

Materials like glass and water are **transparent**. This means light can travel through them. **Opaque** materials are things that do not let any light through at all.

Most materials, such as **metal** and cardboard, are opaque. You cannot see through them.

Translucent materials let some light through, but not all of it. You cannot see clearly through translucent objects.

Translucent materials are slightly see-through, but not completely. Which of these objects are translucent?

FACT CAT FACT

Light bends when it travels through water. This makes objects look like they are broken above and below the surface of the water.

SHADOWS

A **shadow** is a dark shape made when light is blocked by an opaque object. When sunlight hits a tree, a building or a person, it casts a shadow.

If the Sun is behind you, your shadow will be in front of you.

Shadows are the same shape as the object blocking the light. If the object moves, the shadow will also move.

If you move or make shapes with your body, your shadow will change in the same way.

FACT CAT FACT

Translucent objects make shadows because they do not let all light through them. Why don't transparent objects make shadows?

SHADOW PATTERNS

Shadows change throughout the day. This is because the size of a shadow depends on where the Sun is in the sky.

The Sun makes long shadows in the morning and short shadows in the middle of the day. Are shadows long or short in the evening?

midday

evening

morning

If you move an object closer to a light source, its shadow gets bigger. If you move the object further away, it gets smaller.

Thousands of years ago, people told the time using shadows that fell on a type of clock called a **sundial**.

Stand between a lamp and a white wall. Make shapes with your hands. See how the shadow changes as you move closer to and further away from the lamp.

SEEING THINGS

When light hits an object, it **reflects**, or bounces, off it. The reflected light enters your eyes. That is how you see things.

When it is dark, your **pupils** get bigger. This lets more light in to help you see better.

pupil

Darkness means there is no light. It is hard to see things in the dark because no light enters your eyes.

Man-made light sources like torches help you see in the dark. What makes the light in a torch work?

FACT CAT FACT

Sunlight is so strong that it can reach 80 metres down into the darkness of the sea. That's as far as 10 buses end to end!

REFLECTIVE SURFACES

Some objects do not make their own light. They reflect light from other sources. Smooth, shiny **surfaces** reflect light better than rough, dull surfaces.

Metal and glass are good light reflectors. The glass in this building reflects the image of trees and other buildings.

Reflective surfaces are very useful. Car **mirrors** let drivers see the road behind them. **Cat's eyes** reflect headlamps at night to light up the road.

This cyclist is wearing a vest with reflective strips to make sure she can be seen. What other light source is she using to stay safe?

FACT CAT FACT

The Moon might look bright, but it does not make its own light. It reflects light from the Sun.

REFLECTIONS

When light bounces off a reflective surface you see a **reflection**. A reflection is a picture of the object on the reflective surface.

A reflection is the same as the real object, but it is back to front. Which arm is the girl using to brush her teeth? Which arm is raised in the mirror?

Light bounces evenly off very smooth shiny surfaces like glass and mirrors. This makes the reflection very clear.

Ripples in the water mean the surface is not completely smooth. This zebra's reflection looks a bit different to the real zebra.

Light is the fastest thing in the universe. It travels at 300,000 km per second.

QUIZ

Try to answer the questions below. Look back through the book to help you. Check your answers on page 24.

1 Which of these is a natural light source?

a) traffic lights

b) a street lamp

c) a star

2 How long does it take sunlight to reach Earth?

a) about 8 minutes

b) about 8 hours

c) about 8 days

3 Transparent materials do not let any light though. True or not true?

a) true

b) not true

4 What happens to a shadow when you move a light source nearer an object?

a) it gets bigger

b) it gets smaller

c) it stays the same size

5 The Moon does not make its own light. True or not true?

a) true

b) not true

6 Which surface reflects light best?

a) a swimming pool

b) a mirror

c) a cardboard box

GLOSSARY

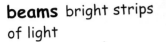

beams bright strips of light

cat's eyes rows of reflectors in the road which reflect headlights when it is dark, to make sure drivers stay on the right side of the road

directions the paths that things move along or the places they point to

light sources things that give out light

lightning flashes of light in the sky during a thunderstorm

man-made describes things that are made by people

materials the substances that objects are made of

metal a hard, shiny substance

mirrors smooth, shiny objects that reflect light well

natural describes things that are found in nature which are not made by people

opaque describes something that does not let any light through

pupils the holes in the centre of your eyes that let in light

reflect when light bounces off an object

reflection the picture formed when light bounces off a smooth surface

screens the front part of televisions and computers

shadow a dark shape created when light is blocked by an object

sundial an old device that uses shadows like the hands of a clock to tell the time

sunlight the light that comes from the Sun

surface the outside layer of something

translucent describes something that lets a bit of light through but not all of it

transparent describes something that lets all light through

INDEX

ANSWERS

Pages 4–21

Page 5: red, orange, yellow, green, blue, indigo and violet

Page 6: a glow worm

Page 8: 150 million kilometres

Page 11: the bag, the marble and the light bulb

Page 13: because they let all light through

Page 14: long

Page 17: batteries

Page 19: a light

Page 20: real – right hand, mirror – left hand

Quiz answers

1 c – a star

2 a – about 8 minutes

3 not true – transparent materials let all light through

4 a – it gets bigger

5 true – it reflects light from the Sun

6 b – a mirror

OTHER TITLES IN THE FACT CAT SERIES...

WAYLAND
www.waylandbooks.co.uk